The Fat Stock Stampede at the Houston Livestock Show and Rodeo

The Fat Stock Stampede at the Houston Livestock Show and Rodeo

by Dotti Enderle

illustrated by Chuck Galey

PELICAN PUBLISHING COMPANY

Gretna 2008

For all the Texas 4-H and FFA members—D. E.

For Judy and Dudley, supporters of the arts—C. G.

*The word "Pelican" and the depiction of a pelican
are trademarks of Pelican Publishing Company, Inc.,
and are registered in the U.S. Patent and Trademark Office.*

Library of Congress Cataloging-in-Publication Data

Enderle, Dotti, 1954-
  The fat stock stampede at the Houston Livestock Show and Rodeo / by
Dotti Enderle ; illustrated by Chuck Galey.
        p. cm.
  Summary: When Jake accidentally unlatches every gate in the row of
pens at the Houston Livestock Show and Rodeo, chaos ensues but with a
bit of ingenuity, Jake finds a way to make things right.
  ISBN 978-1-58980-443-2 (hardcover : alk. paper) [1. Rodeos--Fiction. 2.
Animals--Fiction. 3. Texas--Fiction. 4. Tall tales.] I. Galey, Chuck, ill. II.
Title.
  PZ7.E69645Fat 2008
  [E]--dc22

                                        2007036895

Printed in Singapore
Published by Pelican Publishing Company, Inc.
1000 Burmaster Street, Gretna, Louisiana 70053

THE FAT STOCK STAMPEDE AT THE HOUSTON LIVESTOCK SHOW AND RODEO

It seemed like a good idea at the time, but ideas always seem good when they're only ideas.

Jake strolled the aisles of the Houston Livestock Show, kicking sawdust as he went. It wasn't the best-smelling place he'd ever been. How could it be? Not one single stall was equipped with soap on a rope or underarm deodorant.

Jake held his nose as he rushed to catch up to his parents. As he hurried, he ran his fingers along the rails of the pens. Bad idea! He didn't realize that he'd managed to unlatch each gate as he strummed along.

Inside Reliant Stadium, Jake enjoyed the bull riders, barrel-racers, and calf-scramblers. Then a strange rumbling shook the seats.

"I believe it's going to storm," his mom said.

Storm it did! Just as a broncobuster came pitching out of Chute 4, a herd of heifers charged through the wall, right behind him.

"Stampede!" the announcer yelled.

Well . . . not exactly. The heifers gathered in the
center of the rodeo ring and played a vigorous
game of volleyball with the broncobuster. "Yee-
haw!" he hollered as he sailed back and forth over
the net.

That's when the popcorn vendors came scream-
ing down the aisles. "Help! Help!" Each one was
completely covered in chickens that pecked every
last kernel of popcorn from their trays.

The scheduled performer, "Handsome" Hank Chipkicker, lived up to his name. "I'm outta here!" he shrieked, grabbing his guitars and kicking his way to his flashy pickup truck. He peeled out, then came to a screeching stop before a blockade of swooning swine. They batted their eyes and snorted sweet kisses at him.

"Everyone stay calm," the announcer announced.

"That's easy for you to say," a rodeo clown yelled. He played a vicious game of tug-o-war with a goat that was trying to eat his baggy pants. When the other goats showed up looking hungry, the clowns quickly stuffed themselves into their clown car and—*beep! beep!*—drove away.

Pandemonium followed. Jake and his parents joined in a different stampede—the rodeo spectators trying to make a break for it. They spilled out of the doors into the open air, only to find that the rodeo carnival had become a regular zoo—calves on carousels, rabbits on roller coasters, pigs on paddleboats!

Two brutish bulls blew steam out of their noses and ears after taking over the Chili Cook-Off and turning it vegetarian. They declared a wild and wooly sheep the first-place winner. He strutted proudly, wearing his blue ribbon.

"You!" a livestock judge yelled while pointing a menacing finger at Jake. "I saw you open the pens!"

"I did all this?" Jake asked himself, looking at the rodeo riot.

That's when he noticed the FFA and 4-H folks sitting in the parking lot, crying and sighing over their lost scholarships. "Now they'll never get an education," Jake thought. He had to do something quick!

Jake snatched a baby rattle from a nearby stroller. He took a giant burlap sack from behind a bunch of boxes. Then he grabbed a couple of darts from a game booth. In no time at all, Jake had transformed himself into a rattlesnake—and not just any rattlesnake, but an enormous Texas rattler! His disguise was perfect.

Jake slithered through the midway, hissing, rattling, and baring his fangs. The gobblers flocked in a fury. The ponies pounded the pavement. And the beefalo boogied as though his tail was on fire. Jake's rattlesnake gimmick was so scary, it even curled the horns on the longhorn steer.

The livestock scattered, racing around the rodeo grounds until they came to a stop at the safest place they knew . . . inside their pens. It seems the world's a better place when someone feeds and protects you. The FFA and 4-H students hustled over to make sure all of their animals were safe and secure.

Jake shed his snake costume and hopped in the car with his mom and dad. There'd be no more rodeo today. Jake was happy that the commotion was over, but he felt a tad guilty as he watched through the back windshield.

Those dusty old trail riders were having a heck
of a time getting their horses off the stadium roof.